1976 BENJAMIN F. FAIRLESS MEMORIAL LECTURES

Library of Congress Catalog Card Number 77-075047
ISBN Number 0-915604-11-6

A View of the Corporate Role in Society

John D. Harper

Carnegie-Mellon University Press

Distributed by Columbia University Press
New York — Guilford, Surrey

The Benjamin F. Fairless Memorial Lectures endowment fund has been established at Carnegie-Mellon University to support an annual series of lectures. An internationally known figure from the world of business, government, or education is invited each year to present three lectures at Carnegie-Mellon under the auspices of its Graduate School of Industrial Administration. In general, the lectures will be concerned with some aspects of business or public administration; the relationships between business and government, management and labor; or a subject related to the themes of preserving economic freedom, human liberty, and the strengthening of individual enterprise—all of which were matters of deep concern to Mr. Fairless throughout his career.

Mr. Fairless was president of United States Steel Corporation for fifteen years, and chairman of the board from 1952 until his retirement in 1955. A friend of Carnegie-Mellon University for many years, he served on the board of trustees from 1952 until his death. In 1959 he was named honorary chairman of the board. He was also a leader and co-chairman of Carnegie-Mellon's first development program, from its beginning in 1957.

John Dickson Harper, a director and retired chairman of the board of Aluminum Company of America, was born in Louisville, Tennessee, April 6, 1910.

When he was 15 years old and still in high school, Mr. Harper obtained a summer job at Alcoa's nearby operations — running an electric truck at $12 a week. He continued to work during school vacations until he received his high school diploma.

When Mr. Harper (whose continuous service with Alcoa began in 1931) became a cooperative student at the University of Tennessee, he alternated between classes and his job in the Alcoa plant, switching from school to plant, and back again every three months. He found time to be a member of R.O.T.C., Pershing Rifles and Tau Beta Pi.

Following his graduation in 1933 with a degree in Electrical Engineering, Mr. Harper went to work handling the complex powerhouse switchboard in one of Alcoa's hydroelectric plants. In less than a year he was a junior staff engineer. Two years later, he was assisting in the design and construction of a new generating station.

During most of his 18 years in Tennessee, Mr. Harper channeled his boundless energy into the elaborate Alcoa power division. His first major assignment was that of chief load dispatcher. In 1943, he became assistant power manager of Alcoa's extensive Tennessee and North Carolina generating facilities. During the next eight years he organized central load dispatching, standardized operating procedures, coordinated operations with the Tennessee Valley Authority, directed development of telemetering equipment, developed maintenance procedures for equipment and oils, and administered power contracts.

When Alcoa decided in 1951 to build a $100 million aluminum smelter at Rockdale, Texas, John Harper was given the responsibility of building and operating it.

At Rockdale, Alcoa was pioneering. Besides erecting a huge reduction plant in an industrially undeveloped area of Texas, Alcoa had decided to generate its power by burning lignite, a subbituminous coal abounding in the area. Before it was fed to the boilers, the lignite would have to be crushed and dried.

Mr. Harper soon found that building a smelter was only

one of his many problems. His engineers had the site preparation under control as bulldozers and carry-alls bit into the earth, getting ready for foundations and scooping an 850-acre lake to store water for the smelter. But preparing the Texans for this upheaval in their landscape and their lives was strictly up to him.

Wearing khakis and driving an inexpensive car, Mr. Harper set out to win friends for Alcoa. He learned who was who among the ranchers, farmers, businessmen and politicians; helped the small town of Rockdale expand to accommodate thousands of construction workers and, later, production employees; purchased property and minerals; negotiated water rights-of-way with landowners along a 12-mile pipeline to the San Gabriel and Little Rivers; and, generally, dispelled fears that Pittsburgh Yankees were out to ruin Texas for a profit.

Mr. Harper pledged to Rockdale's town council that Alcoa would pay taxes in advance, so the town could expand such essential municipal facilities as water lines and streets. There also had to be new schools for children who would come with the employment flood. When he learned that the weekly *Rockdale Reporter* had been campaigning for years for a municipal swimming pool, Mr. Harper arranged for Alcoa to donate the land, then pay half the cost of a first-class installation.

Scarcely a year after ground was broken, the first potline at Rockdale Works was producing aluminum on interim electricity purchased from Texas Power & Light. By early 1954, the entire smelter was in operation under its own steam with a capacity of 90,000 tons a year — a figure which expansion has increased to 285,000 tons to make Rockdale Alcoa's largest smelter.

On April 24, 1954, more than 700 special guests, including Gov. Shivers and Alcoa executives, visited the smelter for lunch and a tour preceding an open house.

The next day, John Harper learned what it meant to invite all of Texas to a public inspection. He and his staff had expected 10,000 visitors, at most. By nightfall, more than 20,000 Central Texans had poured through the plant, leaving an exhausted staff.

In 1955, Alcoa management decided John Harper had

fulfilled his Rockdale mission and transferred him to Pittsburgh as assistant general manager of the smelting division.

Mr. Harper progressed rapidly in Pittsburgh. He became smelting division general manager in 1956; assistant production manager in 1960; and, later the same year, vice president in charge of the smelting and fabricating divisions. In 1962, he was elected vice president in charge of production, then executive vice president and a director. He became president in 1963 and chairman of the board in 1970. He has been chairman of the board's executive committee since 1966 and was chief executive officer from 1965 until March 1, 1975. On June 19, 1975, he retired as chairman but continued as a director and chairman of the executive committee.

High among his projects was the Alcoa Smelting Process, a revolutionary, power-saving method of producing aluminum which took 15 years and $25,000,000 to develop.

During his busy years with Alcoa, John Harper got up at 6:30 or earlier every morning, including Sundays and holidays, and his tremendous drive kept him going until late at night.

It was commonplace for him to work several hours in his Pittsburgh office, dash off to New York in a company plane for a business luncheon or other engagement, and be back in late afternoon. By dawn the next day, he could be off to Washington, an Alcoa installation on either coast, or to an overseas business conference.

His leadership in Alcoa was on a practical plane. He delegated authority; expected, and got, results. On major problems, he might ask advice from a dozen associates. But when it was time to act, he made the decision.

Mr. Harper spoke frankly with employees, making sure they had the knowledge necessary to do a good job. He once warned in an internal filmed report: "One mistake — one piece of carelessness in the mill or one goof-up in the shipping department — can cost us thousands of dollars in sales. We lose the business and our competitors get it."

Of all his convictions, none is more positive than his belief that no business can survive without adequate profits — no matter how prosperous it or the country may appear to be.

To the Dallas Management Association, he expressed his feelings this way:

"Whatever the reasons may be, it is evident that increasing numbers of Americans seem to want the benefits of the free enterprise economic system without first putting forth the effort to earn the profits that make possible an even higher standard of living.

"If we are to have a public policy of prosperity without profit, this means that we must embrace a new economic and political philosophy — one in which state control and dictatorial power replace our free choice in the marketplace — and I firmly believe that this is not what Americans, including those in labor and management, really want.

"The dangerous illusion of profitless prosperity feeds on ignorance, indifference and procrastination. . . "

He called business to a wider fulfillment of its social responsibility, and to deeper involvement with the society at large.

To the Congress of American Industry sponsored by the National Association of Manufacturers, he said:

"A viable society in which business can prosper and grow, the kind of society all of us want, demands the intelligent exercise of public responsibility by the business community itself. . .

"It makes sense to participate — with corporate money, talent and energy — in a community project to improve conditions in the slums. In the long run, such participation will prove to be beneficial to your own business. Because, if you reduce delinquency, crime and illiteracy, you reduce your own corporate tax load, and you convert welfare cases into productive workers."

His words and actions have established John Harper as a leader among businessmen in America, and throughout the world, particularly in the aluminum industry.

He is past chairman of The Business Roundtable, and the International Primary Aluminum Institute, vice chairman of the Committee for Economic Development, past president of The Aluminum Association and a senior member of The Conference Board. He is a director of Mellon National Corporation, Metropolitan Life Insurance Company, The Goodyear Tire and Rubber Company, Procter & Gamble Company and Communications Satellite Corporation (COMSAT). He is vice chairman of the Committee for Constructive Consumerism, vice chairman and a life trustee of Carnegie-Mellon University and a member of the Executive Committee of the national council of the Boy Scouts of America.

Mr. Harper is a Fellow of the American Institute of Electrical Engineers and American Society of Mechanical Engineers, and a life member of the Institute of Electrical and Electronic Engineers, Inc. He holds the honorary doctor of engineering degree from Lehigh University, Maryville College and Rensselaer Polytechnic Institute, doctor of laws from the University of Evansville, doctor of science from Clarkson College of Technology and doctor of commercial science from Widener College. His honors also include the Knight's Cross, Order of St. Olav (Norway).

1976

A View of the
Corporate Role in Society

thirteen

A View of the
Corporate Role in Society

I. The Changing Society

Introduction

I am very grateful to the trustees of Carnegie-Mellon University for their invitation to present the Benjamin Fairless Lectures for 1976. It is particularly a privilege to have this part in keeping the memory of such a distinguished and respected leader of American enterprise.

Ben Fairless is remembered, among those who knew him, for many fine and inspiring qualities which set him apart, as a manager and as a man. Yet he is also remembered with admiration by a far wider audience who knew him only through the example which he set. When he believed vital principle to be at stake in the public arena, he did not follow the passive course; rather, he went into the arena himself, there to confront the challenges with uncommon personal courage and characteristic personal force. His efforts strengthened the fabric of our system and his example remains a standard for these times now.

Under the provisions establishing these lectures, the speaker is given considerable latitude in the choice of subject. The focus may be on the internals of corporate management; it may center on the externals of relations with government and labor; or, if he wishes, the speaker may deal with a theme relating to preservation of "economic freedom, human liberty or individual enterprise."

Out of my own experience as a corporate officer and manager, I regard these subjects as inseparable. Over a span of some 50 years with the Aluminum Company of America, I have been privileged to serve in managerial positions from the most junior to the most senior. At every station, the realities are much the same. Successful performance internally rests upon successful performance externally and vice versa. In all instances, success is contingent upon deriving strength from, and imparting strength to, the climate and cause of economic freedom, human liberty and individual enterprise.

This underscores a basic perspective. In our society and

under our system, the corporate role is never static; it is always sensitive to the complex and changing relationships between the society, the corporation and the manager. It is on these interrelationships that I want to focus my remarks during these three presentations.

Under the general theme of "A View of the Corporate Role in Society," I shall consider "The Changing Society," "The Changing Corporation," and "The Changing Manager."

Let me begin by recalling from my own experience a period quite relevant to all that I shall say.

I entered into the management structure of Alcoa in the mid-1930's. Primed with an engineering degree from the University of Tennessee, I was mostly interested in working with electric power. Had I been more aware of the strong currents pulsing through those times, I might well have questioned the long-term wisdom of entering the employ of a large corporation at that time.

As I understand now better than I understood then, the private corporation in America was under siege. For many years, business had enjoyed preeminence as perhaps the most trusted and respected of secular institutions. There had been a period of challenge around the turn of the century but during the 1920's, business appeared to recover its prestige and trust. With the coming of the 1930's, that changed abruptly. Over the first half of the decade, the society seemed to turn upon the corporation and the private business system.

Politics suddenly became more and more demanding and less and less understanding. The government in Washington — with which business previously had almost no relation — seemed to be coming through every corporate door and window, with its agents peering over every executive shoulder. Virtually every mail delivery brought new forms and regulations from agencies and offices of which no one had ever heard. For the managers of the day, it was as though their world had unaccountably gone mad.

That was by no means all. The ethics of managers and the morality of the system were held up to scorn. Critics railed against business values. The private corporation, we began to hear, could no longer be entrusted with its own planning. There were demands for others to sit at the board table. Many voices called for new alternatives to the corporate system. The dialogue filled with confident predictions that the corporation would soon be replaced as the system's central institution. In support of this, the then-new technique of opinion polling found broad public support for government to take over much of the private business function.

There seemed to be no prospect for stemming this tide. If there were a future for the corporation, that future could not be readily discerned. The question seemed to be when, not whether, we would all be working for the state.

While that was 40 years ago, the parallels with the present are apparent. Almost all the words I have used to describe the middle years of the 1930's could be spoken with little revision to describe the middle years of the 1970's.

Once again the corporation is challenged. Once again, politics, government and the courts are demanding. Once again, critics are calling for alternatives to the corporation's place and role in our society. Certainly now, as much as then, there are serious questions, troubling questions, about the future, for that future is not easy to discern.

I fully share the concerns which trouble so many citizens, in and out of business. The public sector's appetite for control over all things private does seem to be ravenous and insatiable. Regulations and restrictions pour forth every day expanding the powers of the state, not only over the large corporation, but over virtually all our private institutions. The impulse toward political management of private lives, private decisions and private institutions is strong and relentless. In truth, we cannot know where or how it may all end.

Yet, in this presentation, it is not my purpose to call upon management to "circle the wagons." Far from it. If I were addressing a corporate audience, my message more nearly would be "let's move 'em out."

Concerned as I am, and as I believe we all should be, about some of the trends now running among us, I do not accept that the end is destined to be so dismal as some project. When I place these times in the context of those earlier times about which I have spoken, I cannot despair; for even though the two periods may run in parallel, it remains that the exact analogy is not there to extend.

Forty years of change — 40 years of change in the society and 40 years of change in the corporation — have made a difference. It is important to the purposes of our discussion to understand this interrelationship — to understand the considerable differences as well as the coincidental similarities between past and present.

In the 1930's, when the balance between private and public sectors were so decisively affected, the society was reacting, in simplest terms, to an absence of change.

The times of the 1920's are remembered now — mostly by those who never knew them — as good times, spirited times, times of Model-T's, flappers and bathtub gin. Underneath that surface, though, there was a deeper — and, I might say, darker — reality.

In a sense that persons under the age of 50 have little basis for comprehending, the 1920's were not times of change. The economic, social and even physical mobility which we know now did not exist then. Our present respect for individual dignity and the worth of human labor was not a common part of the values dominant in the industrial community. Factory work could be, and all too often was, grim, demeaning and hazardous. Life in the worker districts and many company towns was typically oppressive. A first visit to a big city, for a small town boy from rural Tennessee, could very nearly induce culture shock. Even more remote were cultures of other nations on other continents.

Overhanging industrial America — and other industrial societies as well — were the values of hundreds, and even thousands, of years past. Those values were unchanged and seemingly unchangeable. All our institutions — not just business — were authoritarian and aloof, largely conducted not to encourage change but to prevent even the thought of change.

Underneath that surface, there was a yearning for change. When the 1930's began with the economic system in collapse and the political system near the same state, that yearning

twenty-one

broke its bonds.

Overnight, almost, the society came to flashpoint. Warning signals of civil conflict were everywhere. In 1937, the year I attained my first managerial position with Alcoa, the nation was placed on edge by the sitdown strikes by workers in Detroit and the Memorial Day Massacre of workers in Chicago. As we should never forget, the forces which welled up in the 1930's were sullen, angry, potentially destructive forces — forces demanding change long denied.

Today, in the 1970's, the nature of the challenge is materially different.

Unlike the times before, we have had change. Since the 1930's, and especially since World War II, we have experienced the most extensive and pervasive change ever known by a human society. The demand we are hearing now is a demand that we cope with change, that we bring together all our capabilities to cope with what these years have wrought.

For myself, I believe this demand is valid.

Our society clearly presents needs which we have not known before. In all our activities, we have come to a new order of complexity and interdependence. Old ways, familiar methods, accepted standards will not suffice. If this society and system are to succeed, standards must rise, tolerances must be drawn more fine, disciplines upon our performance in all areas must become more exacting. Today, quite as much as when our Republic began, we must think anew and act anew if we are to realize the fullness of our potential.

Here lies both the promise and the peril for the society and the corporation.

Forty years ago, our institutions were largely set against change. That was true of politics, government and the courts; it was true of other institutions, too. It was all too often true of much of business. Despite the promise of human betterment afforded by the Industrial Revolution, despite the great potential implicit in the new inventions and technologies emerging in the century's early decades, the society still had no instrumentality for achieving change and diffusing the benefits widely among the people.

Out of the fires of the Thirties, though, such an instrumentality was found in the private business corporation. With its flexibility, with its capacity for innovation, with its capability for changing itself, the corporation became an instrument for achieving much of what the society sought. In consequence, corporation and society have moved in tandem since, seeking out and satisfying society's needs and wants and moving on to undertake other challenges.

That has been a remarkable relationship. Since mid-century, at least, the relationship between the American society and the American corporation has been as creative, productive and successful as any history has ever known.

That is the promise of the moment. If today's demands are new and difficult, it remains that the private corporation is uniquely suited to serve — to continue serving — as agent of the society's private aspirations. Yet it is in the continuation of this relationship that there presently lies peril.

Our traditions have cast the public and private sectors into an adversary relationship. The crucial interdependence between both sectors is not always maturely and responsibly acknowledged on either side. As a result, that relationship is always vulnerable — vulnerable to ignorance and folly, vulnerable especially to demagoguery. That is the particular danger of this period now.

If we are to cope with change, if we are to find our way through what the years ahead present, public sector and private sector need to come to new understandings, new accommodations, a new sort of relationship. That requires adjustment on both sides.

As I have seen at every station in my career, the great enemy of business in the public sector is ignorance. All too often the most menacing proposals in the political arena stem not from willful intent to inflict injury as much as from unawareness of how serious the injury might be. Our contemporary politics is far more understanding of the ecology of forests and fowl and fishlife than it is of the no less sensitive ecology of the enterprise system. That lack of understanding is, ultimately, as injurious to the political sector as to the corporate sector.

While it is not asking too much to ask greater political sensitivity for the essentials of corporate survival, neither is it too much to ask for greater business sensitivity to the essentials of politics and government.

The adversary relationship has not been prolonged solely by ignorance and misunderstanding in the public sector. All too many on the business side are insensitive to and even unmindful of realities on the governmental and political side. It has never been and will never be realistic, desirable or possible to conduct the affairs of a system so complex and interdependent as ours without a central role being taken by government. While neither business nor the people need or want more government, both the people and business very much need better government — government better informed, better motivated, better conducted than now.

So long as the relationship remains adversary in nature, it will be vulnerable to demagoguery. That is a particular concern at this period.

Recent years have brought into our dialogue what can only be described as demagoguery directed against business. Certainly the corporation and corporate management do not and should not enjoy any immunity from external criticism; such criticism can, in fact, be a source of strength. But all too much of the popular outcry now raised against business goes beyond objective critique; it represents a style and purpose, an effort to reignite and rekindle the flames which so greatly threatened this society in years past. It is as much a peril now as then. Citizens of constructive purpose in all sectors must be on guard against those who by intent or ignorance would use spurious issues and incendiary rhetoric to set the society against the system which sustains it and supports its wholesome change.

The private relationship between this society and the corporations which function for it is a shelter for our freedom and individual liberties and a shield against perversion of our governing values. Before the political system can be radically changed, the people must be divided from — or against — the business system. We must recognize this and, in so doing, recognize demagoguery as the menace and danger that it is for society as a whole.

Wherever we can, however we can, we need to work together to transform the relationship between society and corporation, between government and business, from adversary status to cooperative and constructive status.

If that is our long term goal, we still face the immediate challenge of a difficult and demanding period. How is business to respond?

As I know from long experience, many managers are inclined to respond to any external challenge by hiring a lawyer, sending in their dues to the NAM and considering their duty done. Dues paying and fee paying won't do it anymore. The manager cannot respond to these times by saying, "I gave at the office." In this arena, it is what we do outside the office that matters.

If that response is unsatisfactory, another familiar response is even more inacceptable. That is the response of those who confuse the chief executive suite with the bridge of a battleship. At the first hint of challenge, they come steaming forth, all guns firing, under the impression that if business will fight long enough and hard enough, government or unions or academic critics will go away and business won't be bothered.

That, too, is a response which won't do anymore.

Over all my working life, I have seen business pay — as it is still paying — an enormous price for the folly of those who cast the business role as a vendetta with society. Let me say, as strongly as I can, that the contest of the times is not a contest between social progress and economic progress.

That is not and has never been true. Our history clearly teaches that social progress is not inimical to economic progress, just as it also teaches that economic progress is not incompatible with social progress. As our own social and economic advance supports, each is imperative to the other.

Thus, as we address this new period, I believe it is particularly important for business to identify carefully the nature of both the present challenges and the responsibilities which those challenges impose.

First, in regard to the challenge, we should reject the insidious notion that society is the enemy. A changing society is never a hostile environment to the corporation so long as the corporation serves responsively as an agent of constructive change.

Second, I believe it is especially necessary that we not confuse all change with social change. What is trying and testing management today is by no means solely the demands arising from politics, government or other external sources. Very great challenges are developing from within the business system itself. Since the start of the decade, many basic premises of management have been significantly and permanently altered by the new realities of inflation, energy, scarcity and complexity. This is no parochially American situation; the change is worldwide and the manager's understanding must be worldwide, too.

Stated simply, today's manager can no longer manage by yesterday's book. To perform the managerial function successfully, the manager must think anew and learn new skills and arts.

This goes, of course, to the matter of the responsibilities which today's challenges impose.

The first responsibility always is the success of the corporation. Only a successful corporation can provide jobs, security, profits and taxes. Only a successful corporation can be effective in helping society cope with change. Only a successful corporation can deserve or have society's respect or trust. We should never forget that it was failure to keep this responsibility which opened the way 40 years ago for imposition of change from without.

Beyond these internal responsibilities, I believe modern management must accept and faithfully keep other responsibilities relating to the external role. I list four such responsibilities.

1. *Management must be responsible for the face of the corporation:* for presenting the corporation as a credible, trustworthy, constructive participant in the times.

2. *Management must be responsible for presenting the corporation's point of view:* the debate regarding the corporate role has become a highly intellectualized debate. Goods and services alone will not win such debates. The corporation must be prepared and able to answer its challenges as articulately as they are presented.

3. *Management must be responsible for alerting all concerned:* the community of interest on any concern within this complex society is far more encompassing than one corporation or one industry — wider even than business itself. When concerns arise, management must be in the forefront of that full community of interest, alerting and organizing it into an effective response.

4. *Finally, management must be responsible for working together for the common good:* the cause of management must be the greatest good for the greatest number. In that spirit, then, management must regard its role and its performance to be affected with a broader interest than ever before.

I realize that these responsibilities go beyond many traditional concepts. They ask the corporate manager to take an out-front role in a society which can and often does exact a price of the out-front leader. If there be risks, though, those risks are only part of the manager's new and necessary role.

As this society attempts to cope with change, the corporation and the corporate manager must be a part of that demanding endeavor.

A decade ago, amid the ferment of the 1960's, I spoke before the National Association of Manufacturers in New

York. At that time, I told my colleagues in management some things I want to repeat here now.

"Responsibility is something each of us must accept. We must use the resources, talents and energies of business widely and effectively to advance the public interest and the system of private enterprise on which it depends. We must accept personal responsibility for our own stewardship as managers of business.

"Great tides of change are on the move today, and the business system of this nation must move with them, must help to direct them through exercising its public responsibility. We cannot shirk or evade that responsibility."

That is still my conviction.

That is why, as I said at the start, my message to my colleagues in business is not, "Circle the wagons" — but is, rather, "Let's get moving."

The times are difficult and exacting. Large forces moving here and around the world are crowding in upon the traditional conduct of corporate affairs. Old assumptions, old standards, old methods, old levels of acceptable performance must change. Simply to keep the corporation running right and running profitably will require managers to acquire and exercise new skill, new competence and new vision.

While the internal demands of the corporation are many and strong, the external demands are insistent and the external constituencies impatient. Once again, a changing society is seeking an instrument to serve its needs for coping with what change has wrought. As a matter of both duty and opportunity, today's manager must take a leading part in the response.

The society and the corporation still have much they can do together while there is little either can do apart. As the history of the modern relationship clearly demonstrates, the private corporation is strengthened, not weakened, by meeting its public responsibilities; by moving with and not against the tides of society's change.

Thus, I say that the true challenge confronting corporate management now is to get moving — get moving on further and broader service to our changing society.

A View of the
Corporate Role in Society

II. The Changing Corporation

II. The Changing Corporation

In the preceding chapter, I concentrated my remarks on the relationship of the corporate role to "The Changing Society." I now want to focus our discussion somewhat differently, this time on the corporate role in relation to "The Changing Corporation."

I believe there is a particular need for this emphasis.

Over the past 40 to 50 years, the corporation has effected a close, productive and commonly beneficial relationship with our society during a period of unparalleled change. That achievement is large. Certainly it is important. Yet it is only in the nature of us all to feel that once such an achievement is wrought, the labor is done.

Change is never done. Diverse as it is, large as it is, volatile as it has been and can be again, our society presents a constant and continuing challenge to the corporation and the community of corporate managers. It is important, therefore, that we be aware not only that there were large and important achievements in the past; it is necessary that we understand how those gains were wrought, for such knowledge may be required again.

Let me illustrate with examples from past and present.

As I depicted in my remarks yesterday, the attacks on business 40 years ago were mounted by a society denied change and determined to have it. In the perceptions prevailing then, the corporation was seen as agent of the status quo. It was not just that the corporation might resist change. The belief was widespread that the corporation could not and would not permit change. Cheap labor, exploitative labor practices, autocratic management — all the aspects in disfavor — were regarded as preconditions for profit under the existing system.

On this popular premise, critics of the corporation argued

that the change society sought could be accomplished only by changing the system.

Needless to say, history has destroyed that argument. Without embracing any of the alternate systems in vogue during the 1930's, the society has achieved unparalleled change — and the corporation has served effectively as the society's instrument. Now, the need is to cope with what has been wrought, to harmonize our gains and strengthen the base for our continuing social and economic progress. Yet, against this clear and present need, critics are raising a new and particularly disruptive argument.

The way to cope with change, so some are saying, is to control the corporation's function as servant of the society's need for change. Inhibit that function, restrict it, make it subject to political consent and change will be coped with by the expedient of being prevented. That motivation underlies the attacks on growth, technology and science, on the diversity of products and services, even on such matters as corporate advertising.

Times change. Arguments change. Goals, though, change little. The objective of the adversaries remains now as it has been always: to alienate the society and the corporation and to exploit that alienation for purposes of changing our traditional business system.

If the corporate community is to address this attack effectively and successfully, it is necessary that we remember and apply the lessons of our own recent past.

I stress this because, in simple truth, the past is not well understood. On both sides, among managers and among critics, there exists an entrenched belief that change occurring in the corporation has been almost entirely imposed from without, principally by and through the government. That is not the case. On the contrary, the very strength and success of corporate change stems from the fact that such change has come, by and large, from within.

This is of importance beyond the corporation itself. Over the past ten years or so, we have been made aware that there are many conflicts and tensions in our society arising from the lack of institutional change. A changing society clearly requires change of all its institutions. Our efforts to achieve that have not always been fruitful. If the unrest and clamor of the 1960's has receded, for the moment, it remains that many of the underlying causes of tension and conflict still exist, largely unabated or unresolved.

Of all our institutions, it is the corporation, virtually alone, which has undergone the most successful change. That change has succeeded because when the corporation was confronted with the demands of a changing society, the corporation undertook to change itself — to change from within rather than forcing change to be imposed from without. On much reflection, I am not certain institutions can be changed in any other way. If institutions are changed from without, by laws or decrees, or by the influence of physical demonstrations and confrontations, they cease to be the same institution; in fact, they cease even to be institutions, becoming, instead, captives and creatures of other forces.

In this context, the corporate example is instructive for all who direct our other private and secular institutions and, especially, for those who administer our public institutions. As cannot be emphasized too strongly, the opinion polls which reflect declining public confidence in business, as an institution, show equal and even greater declines in trust for other institutions as well. If we are to restore trust and confidence as a strength of this society, if we are to assure the necessary autonomy of our institutions, managers and administrators must allow the forces of change to work within or else other forces will surely work from without to compromise and, in time, to capture those institutions which we value.

Whatever the source, whether political, governmental, judicial or otherwise, management from without is inevitably destructive of any institution. The tendency toward such management from without is a trend to be resisted not only in business but in our universities and schools, our cities and states, even in such sensitive institutions as church and family.

thirty-five

To trace the course of change for the corporation, it is necessary to go back to the beginning. The corporate form is very old. In Europe and England, its uses long predate the Industrial Revolution. Under the practices of that ancient past, private corporations were very private holdings of individuals or families or other limited interests. In a sense largely beyond comprehension today, to work for a corporation, at any level, was to work for, at the pleasure of, and solely to the gain of its owners. The worker had little, if any, identity and few, if any, rights as a citizen apart from the corporation; with retirement unknown and unthinkable, the corporation was the sum of the worker's existence from childhood to the grave.

With the coming of the Industrial Revolution in this country, those ancient traditions transferred into our culture, too, barely ameliorated by any political enlightenment. The working class here could and did find some escape into the opening lands of our spacious continent. For those who could not escape, their circumstances and conditions, even in early Twentieth Century America, were still too much like those prevailing in Seventeenth and Eighteenth Century Europe.

The arrangements were beyond questioning. This was the way it had always been; this was the way it was supposed to be. What some described as "the natural order," was simply assumed to be beyond change.

On these shores, though, other forces were at work. Political democracy. The vote. Education. Continental expansion. Invention and technology. All these forces and more were changing the potential and the prospects for the human condition.

The owners of the corporation — those who put down the base for America's great industrial surge — deserve their full due. Harnessing the resources of an undeveloped continent, putting in place the engine of our industrial drive, required large ability and broad vision; they had such qualities in abundance. In this sense, they were anything but agents of the status quo.

Out of the proprietary tradition, though, there evolved a mortal myopia. However large their vision of mills and plants and bridges and railroads, they often could not see — and did not know they should see — the human beings who made those visions succeed.

If they were enlarging the horizons of the nation, they were, all too often, contracting the horizons and the hopes of the workers. In human terms, the practices of the day were hurtful and harmful to people and to society as a whole. As agents, witting or unwitting, of an unacceptable social status quo, the owners were set in conflict with the forces stirring in the cause of social change.

By the 1930's, the controlling interests of the corporation faced a stark but unmistakeable choice: they could hold to their traditional beliefs about society or they could hold their corporations, but they could not hold both. Unless the emerging values of the society became the controlling values of the corporation, change would be imposed from without. The private corporation would cease to be the same institution it had always been, and would become, instead, an organ of the state.

Change had to come — and it did. It did not come by any act of Congress or the courts; neither did it come by any sweeping act on the part of the corporate owners. Successful change never comes with a sudden bolt of lightning and thunderclap; much like a seed, it germinates, it puts down roots, then, over a long process, it grows, flowers and bears fruit.

Change in the corporation has grown in the manner of the seed. Owners and managers of another time perceived that the private corporation could not stand in the strong winds and shifting sands of the Twentieth Century unless it put down deep roots in the society itself. What we have seen flower and bear fruit since, in terms of the closer and more successful relationship between corporation and society, is fulfillment of that wisdom.

Let me offer several illustrations of this process and how it worked.

thirty-seven

- Over almost all our history, the impulses of this society have been determinedly democratic. Since the 1930's, especially, this has been one of the strongest forces running among us. The corporation has greatly strengthened its relationship by falling in step with this irreversible trend.

The first and, in many ways, still the most important step taken by the corporation is the democratization of ownership. The dispersal of share ownership — among managers, employees, individuals, families and, especially, the many trusts on which Americans depend for personal security — has been a revolution in itself. In all history, the corporation has never been so widely owned as now. The roots of corporate ownership run both wide and deep and that affords strength which the corporation has never previously enjoyed.

Along with the democratization of ownership, the corporation moved to democratize its management. The corporation has opened itself to managers chosen and advanced on the basis of ability, rather than on the basis of ownership or ancestry. In so doing, the corporation has drawn upon a far broader reservoir of the society's talents and abilities, and, in the process, it has drawn closer to the pulsebeat of the society itself.

The effects are pervasive within the corporation itself. Internally, today's private corporation is vastly different from the rigidly stratified organization of the past. From the lunch line in the company cafeteria to the reception room in the executive suite, the corporate milieu is far more open, casual and comfortable, far more reflective of the society's own predominant character. In fact, it is not insignificant that of the society's public and private institutions, the corporation tends to be, typically, the most democratic of all.

- As the corporation has responded to the impulses of democracy, so it has also been responsive to this society's extraordinary demand for openness. At the time of World

War I, Woodrow Wilson appealed to all nations for "Open covenants openly arrived at." In so doing, he spoke for an old and strong American trait: distrust of decisions reached in secret behind closed doors. By tradition and practice, though, the early corporation ranked among the most closed, most secretive of organizations; as with much else, such secrecy was considered an essential of corporate success. Not only was information closely guarded from outside eyes and ears, it was closely held within as well.

Today, that is no longer the reality. While all private organizations have need for privacy about various aspects of their operations, the corporation has become far more open, both within and without. Better management is one direct result. By falling in step with the society, though, the corporation has become, perhaps, society's most open institution, certainly more so than the institutions of the public sector. What the individual citizen can know or learn about the conduct of the modern corporation far surpasses what he is likely to know or learn about the affairs of the typical public agency.

• Since earliest times in colonial America, another trait of the American character has been a jealous concern for the welfare of the community. Such a concern was alien to the corporate tradition. Other considerations, rather than consideration for the community, controlled corporate decisions and policies. When the society began to assert its new will and values, the corporation found itself weak at its very base; corporate unconcern for the community was reciprocated by community unconcern for the corporation. Once again, the corporation chose to fall in step.

My own development as a manager was shaped by the responsibilities which fell to me in the field to establish and maintain better community relations in my areas of responsibility. We learned then that it was not enough for the corporation to favor the community with its presence and its payroll. There had to be attention to the tensions always present between town people and plant people.

thirty-nine

There had to be concern for the corporate impact upon community services and resources. There had to be attention to the face which the corporation presented to the community.

When corporate priorities moved out of phase with the community pace, we paid our taxes early. When plant operations required construction of a lake, we did not surround it with a nine-foot steel wire fence to keep the public out; we stocked it with bass and invited the community in, to share it and enjoy it as their own. We tried to be, in every way, concerned and caring citizens of the community; in so doing, we were falling in step with the society.

• Of all the accommodations between corporation and society, none was more important than the change still evolving between management and labor. As I have suggested, the traditions of the corporate past, back to ancient times, allowed little thought of the worker in individual terms.

Older cultures had simply accepted that property rights were paramount over individual rights. Our society, though, could not — and did not — accept that dictum. Out of that conflict of values, management and labor were thrown into a grim and unyielding adversary relationship. That relationship cost us dearly — and its residue costs us still. Nonetheless, over time, both of the adversaries began to fall in step.

Slowly, minds opened and communication opened. Corporate leaders and union leaders alike began to recognize that most of their interests were common interests. Out of this, there has come — and is still coming — a growth of mutual understanding and cooperation. In today's perceptions, we recognize the worker not as an enemy but as a strength of the corporation and the corporate system. As is said abroad, the difference between European and American attitudes is that, in Europe, the worker loves the boss and hates the system; while in America, the worker hates the boss and loves the system.

I'd like to emphasize a point — that I am not selling labor organizations — they can be very expensive. But with enlightened leadership, labor and management can look to their common interests.

- I could continue this listing on at great length. At so many points, the corporation has become the principal instrument for satisfying the society's needs and fulfilling its aspirations. It has moved in step with society's movements. By that closeness, it has become more a part of the society, served the society better and earned, in return, society's crucial trust.

Out of this recital, there is a point I wish to underscore.

Forty years ago, it was held as a fixed belief of the corporate tradition that change in the society should be regarded as antagonist and enemy of the corporate success. That belief has yielded only begrudgingly. In some quarters, still, the notion lingers that such change is inimical to corporate interests.

What I have related here plainly says the opposite. After decades of change — the most relentless and pervasive change ever experienced by any society — the corporation is not less successful, it is not less respected, its place is not less secure. On the contrary, by putting down its roots, by embracing the society's values as its own, by moving with the society as the society has moved, the corporation is greatly strengthened.

Society has allowed enlargement of the corporate role. It functions now as the central provider of goods and services and jobs. It is the cornerstone of personal security for families and individuals. It is an integral part of virtually all the mainline endeavors to improve the quality of life in our communities, large and small. Where, 40 years ago, it might have seemed a contradiction to speak of the "changing corporation," today "change" and "corporation" fit together as virtual synonyms.

Old notions and old attitudes, though, die slowly. It remains embedded in parts of the corporate mentality that social change is antagonist and enemy. On the basis of that conditioning, there comes the reflex now for managers to turn and stand — stand against social change. It is on that point that I want to emphasize my own purely personal view.

In terms of standing and fighting for essential business positions and principles, I believe I have, as they say, paid my dues. At every stage, I have tried to practice the principles of management responsibility which I preach. I have presented the company point of view. I have acted within the larger sphere to alert all concerned. I have devoted myself to bringing others together to work together for the common good.

I believe, though, that we must carefully keep our focus. It is the duty of management to fight tirelessly against encroachments from any source upon the necessary rights and prerogatives of private ownership and management. It is a misconception, though, to place the corporation in contention with the society over the society's own changing and evolving values.

What we must recognize, more clearly than we do, is that the corporation no longer functions solely as an economic institution. It functions, at least equally, as a social institution. The standards of management — and of individual managers — must take this clearly into account.

This is where the challenge lies. Our society is by no means done with its own change. We have need, as I suggested earlier, to cope with change, to harmonize our gains, to make our complex and increasingly interdependent system function more rationally and more successfully. Yet this in no way implies that we should undertake to stop change; those who ask that are speaking medieval nonsense, asking us to turn against and deny the advance of knowledge itself.

The gains of the last half century have only served to open broader horizons for us all. As a people, we can think now of change beyond our reach or reference in times past. To achieve the kind and quality of life we need, want and can have for all our people requires continuing change — and that is the continuing role of the corporation.

To cope with the problems begotten by change, this society must have much more innovation. Government, as an institution, is proving to be inadequate in this respect. Quite obviously, the private corporation is presented with both an opportunity and a duty to serve, as it has in the past, as a center of such innovation.

The horizons of the corporation, though, are not all close by. I believe we need to stress that if this society is to live amicably and at peace, we must move into a new and much closer relationship with the world. Here, in particular, the role of the corporation is crucial.

As there are those calling mindlessly for an end to change at home, so there are those who call upon us to become a hermit society, withdrawing from the world. Such counsel is folly. Commerce between nations is the only sure and solid basis for international accord. In the years immediately ahead, great responsibility rests upon our corporate management to look to horizons beyond these shores. Abroad, as at home, the corporation must be a part of putting into place the necessary base to feed, clothe, house and usefully employ peoples everywhere. That base is, in turn, the essential base for understanding, accord and peace among nations.

On all fronts, the corporation is called to continue and to enlarge its role of service. Yet one reality should be kept clearly in focus. There is no higher social responsibility for corporate managers than the return of an adequate profit by producing needed goods and services at an acceptable price. Profit and profit alone sustains the corporation as an institution. As the corporation assumes a larger and more crucial role as a social institution, adequate profit assumes larger and more crucial social importance.

In my student days, long ago, we used to hear much about the inequity of our legal tradition which conferred upon the corporation status, under the law, as a person. The old populist traditions of my native South regarded that as the root of much evil, for it gave to the corporation rights usurped from the people themselves.

That line of argument is not much heard now. It is not heard because it is no longer so relevant. The rights of the corporation are not greatly reduced, but the rights of the people are greatly increased. That is as it should be and must be.

Yes, of course, regulation, oversight, intrusions of every kind from the outside are restrictive, they are burdensome. Yet such restrictions are not nearly so burdensome upon the corporation as is or would be the loss of the society's trust. By changing itself, the corporation has earned and received the society's trust; as society continues to change, the corporation, too, must continue to change. That is the critical role of the corporation in our time and place.

A View of the
Corporate Role in Society

III. The Changing Manager

porate role is defined in this fashion, I believe it is apparent that the corporate function is, in the highest sense, a public function.

That introduces into our thinking a changing conception of managers. In all that the manager does, in all that he decides, in all the contacts he makes within and without, the manager is functioning to a great extent in a public capacity.

In such a public capacity, the corporate manager inevitably becomes subject personally to the kinds of standards and tests of public scrutiny which apply to our public officers. In other words, the manager has constituencies to serve and satisfy; he cannot claim sanctuary from public contact or public questioning about his performance. Our standards must take this into account. How a manager handles his internal tasks, how he handles his external relations, how he handles the exposition of company policy, how he handles himself in the public eye — all are factors which must enter into evaluation of the modern manager.

If we are to qualify and develop managers by these changing concepts, what tests and standards should apply? It is a prerogative of service as a chief executive officer to be able to formulate one's own private answers to such questions — and I want to share with you my own personal list of the attributes I believe a manager must have and the qualities which he must develop.

As a starting point, it is, of course, fundamental that those entering management must be competent for the technical and professional tasks assigned. The managerial role rests on that. Yet it is implicit in the term "manager" that the duties require management of people. To fulfill those duties, it is prerequisite that managers be capable of empathizing with others, of being sensitive to people, of being able and willing to communicate with people. These are not universal qualities. *Senior management,* though, needs to be discerning in identifying the presence — or the absence — of such qualities among those entering the management force.

As the manager moves within the corporate structure, there are other qualities to be acquired and developed. Basic again, at every level, is a good technical knowledge of the company's operations and its products. That knowledge must increase and broaden directly in proportion to the manager's position on the executive level. Along with advancement and enlarging responsibility, the manager needs — and must develop — a sense of history: history of his industry and company, of community and region, of nation and world — and above all, sense of the history of the system in which he serves. The manager who lacks that perspective lacks understanding of who he is and what he is about as a manager or as a citizen.

These basics form the platform for what is clearly the most important of managerial functions: that is, communication. Whether dealing internally or externally, the manager must be able to communicate, easily and readily. He must be able, with equal ease, to handle questions and to convey ideas. The manager ill-at-ease with ideas is a manager out of place in these times.

In the concept I am offering, though, it should be said that communication is not to be confused with command. With every directive there should be an accompanying "why." This is an essential and basic difference between the corporation of today and the corporation of yesterday. Whether in contacts on the shop floor or in the bargaining of union negotiations, the key to improving relations with labor is willingness to explain why. To all its constituencies, internal and external, management must be ready to tell where the company is, where it is going — and why that goal is a goal in the common interest.

Let me add this one further observation. I believe and strongly advocate that managers must speak up and speak out to all their many audiences. While they should be articulate participants in the dialogue, there is an implicit need to be attentive listeners, too. Communication is never a one-way process: before we speak, we need to listen, for the best communicators are nearly always the best listeners.

As the manager moves on to the higher levels of the corporate structure, he must recognize and accept a broadening range of responsibility. In his own area, he must take a solid and constructive role in contributing to the formation of company policy. Once policy is decided upon, he must accept a high order of responsibility for articulating it effectively and intelligently both internally and externally.

In fulfilling the trust of higher levels of management, it becomes especially important to learn to identify and cope responsibly with the outside influences bearing on the corporation's performance and purpose. Outside influences are today decisive influences upon the lives and work of the people within the corporation. The ranking managers must be able to relate those influences to the jobs and to the people of the organization.

Employees are the strength of the corporation. For them, the corporation must be, very simply, a good place to work. A sensitive part of making any place a good place to work is the exercise of the managerial responsibility for informing employees about the meaning and effects of external influences.

What about the position at the top: that is, the position of the chief executive officer? I do not adhere to the school which holds that responsibilities and involvements diminish while leisures and pleasures increase at the top of the corporate structure. Quite the contrary, responsibility increases on an ascending scale. The chief executive officer must accept more responsibility simply because he has more responsibility, more influence, and more resources at hand to discharge his trust.

The CEO's first responsibility, of course, is to be certain the organization is right: staffed right, running right, planning right. He must be sure that there is proper financing, adequate machinery and a prudent supply of the raw materials required. He must be sure that the corporation is properly fulfilling its mission to all its constituents. He must be sure that a high standard of ethics is promulgated and enforced in the corporation in all its actions. These things are basic. On beyond such fundamentals, the CEO bears responsibility for things external. In this function, it is not enough

fifty-one

for him merely to hire others to cope with the outside influences and concerns. Such externals may be new, they may be complex, they may be difficult. If that newness, complexity and difficulty is beyond the competence of the man at the top, then both he and the organization he heads are in trouble.

The CEO in today's corporation must be able to relate complex concerns, one to another, and to understand the interrelationships of those concerns within his company. He should, as well, be able to do the same in identifying the relationships and commonality of interests between his company and other companies.

If the corporation is people, as we say, then it follows that the people comprising the corporation should be broadly representative of the diversity and richness of the society's human resources. That representation should never be left to government compulsion. On the contrary, management should be far ahead of government, ahead of society itself, in seeking out new talents for the organization as a whole and for its managerial ranks in particular.

What I am saying on this underscores a larger point. Over the period of which I have been speaking, business has turned its course — turned away from standards and values which could no longer be sustained or defended and turned toward practices and purposes much more consistent with society's higher goals and better qualities. This movement has not all come under duress or compulsion. Quite often, in fact, corporations have moved ahead of society and certainly ahead of government.

Since early in the century, for example, corporations, in many instances, have been in the forefront of efforts to protect and improve our environment and conserve our resources. To cite one instance, it was initiative from corporate leadership in this city — through the Allegheny Conference — that helped to clear the air and clean the rivers to make Pittsburgh a more livable place. That has been the case in city after city across the nation.

In similar fashion, the corporation has been in the

forefront of much other constructive change. Corporations pioneered the great efforts to improve the health and safety of workers, to strengthen the financial security of workers and their families, to place higher education within the reach of all. Long before the word "consumerism" had ever been heard, corporations were vigorously competing to identify customer needs, measure customer reactions, respond to customer complaints. As is sometimes forgotten, product warranties were not invented in Washington, but were conceived and put into service by private corporations first.

Over the span of my own experience, there has been an impressive advance in the level of corporate ethics. The dog-eat-dog morality of other times is gone — and, I say, good riddance. In place of that, there has grown a broad and genuine concern for setting and maintaining high standards of ethical conduct in all areas of corporate relations.

I believe it is accurate to say that our directions, generally, are good. In most areas, the modern corporation has turned on the right course. Where the concern lies, and where the trouble arises, though, is with the distance we have traveled — or, perhaps, I should say, the distance we have yet to travel.

Whether in hiring and promotion practices, in protecting the environment, in satisfying the consumer, in applying and practicing higher ethical standards, or in any of a number of other areas, we must be sensitive to the needs and desires of society, and we must make continued strides in satisfying those needs and desires.

Certainly, business has made and is making great contributions to our society. The American people, I believe, are well aware of that, well aware of the great changes which have been made within business since 40 years, 20 years or 10 years ago. What the people are asking of managers now is a question which public figures have become much more accustomed to hearing: it is the old question, "What have you done for us lately?"

Unlike some of my contemporaries, I happen to think that it is a fair question which it is perfectly proper for the society to ask. One cannot drive back and forth each day to

fifty-three

corporate office or classroom without recognizing that there are obvious, visible, tangible shortfalls on the American promise. Without waiting for others to raise the question, managers themselves should be the first to ask, what have we in business done lately, what are we doing now, to overcome the problems which abound?

I realize that it is an old tradition in business to answer with arguments — with advertisements and speeches and films and economic education programs on which so much energy is spent. Undoubtedly, there is some value in this. Over my experience, though, I have seen American business lose a great many arguments in politics, government and courtroom, but I have seldom seen anyone argue very successfully with what American business achieves when it really goes into action.

For today's managers — and tomorrow's — the meaning is apparent. With little help, managers can muster many arguments with and against the change welling up in this society. Worthy arguments are certainly worth making. Surely, though, the history of the last half century teaches that the more effective answer is for the manager to act in response to the times.

There is much we could be and should be doing outside the corporation. I believe, personally, that we ought to be making the most vigorous attack upon unemployment in our inner cities. Over the past few years, I have been particularly gratified by the success of the National Alliance of Businessmen in finding jobs and putting inner city people into constructive work. NAB programs over the past 8-1/2 years have provided jobs for 2-1/4 million disadvantaged adults, almost 900,000 Viet Nam veterans and 35,000 ex-offenders. The NAB also has supported programs that provided 1,700,000 summer jobs for inner-city young people. This is an achievement which government alone has not been able to match. That is only one program; there ought to be many more bringing the resources of business directly to bear on the clear and apparent social concerns of these times.

On this, though, let me raise a caution. When the manager

sets out to relate with the society, it is not necessary to go into the inner city or to city hall or to Washington — or to any other distant place. The central corporate relationship with society occurs within the corporate walls; virtually every corporate decision and practice, every contact with shareholders, employees, suppliers and customers, ultimately has effect upon society and upon the corporation's standing in the society's esteem and respect. This is an important perspective.

If we listen attentively to the voices of society, I think we will appreciate where change within the corporation is overdue. Work needs redefining, products need redesigning, methods need revising, goals and purposes and attitudes most certainly need reviewing — if we are to keep the corporation in step with our changing society.

This only emphasizes my basic theme. Anytime we encounter troublesome new demands and challenges, we are inclined to look for enemies who may be causing the clamor. There is much of that now. Yet what I am saying is this:

Government is not the enemy. Society is not the enemy. Environmentalists, consumerists, unionists, youth — these are not enemies. Certainly change is not the enemy. For the corporation, as for all our institutions, the enemy is within. It is in our own narrowness and parochialism, in our own complacency and isolation, that the real enemy lies. It is against this enemy that the manager must exert the greatest effort.

Over the course of these lectures, I realize that I have expressed some views not always typical of the corporate community. If not, the choice is deliberate. Out of the experiences which have shaped my views, I simply have not come to share the perception that businessmen need to be gloom-mongers about the future of business or naysayers about the demands of society.

One such experience came at the start of the 1940's, when I was called to my first major responsibility as a manager within Alcoa. From the course of world events, it was foreseeable that this nation, this system and the freedoms we cherish were moving toward confrontation with the forces of the totalitarians. We knew that test would require vastly greater production of aluminum, but first there would be needed far more electric energy. I was given responsibility for assuring the availability of that energy for our largest operation.

The story of how we succeeded against long odds and large obstacles is only a small detail to the greater national effort — and that is not the story I mean to tell. That assignment, though, came at a crucial time for me.

Until then, as a young manager, I had been in the milieu of others who were lamenting and resisting change, confident that the society and the system were going down the drain because of it. It would have been very easy for me to follow in their path, to have spent my life as a negative and non-contributing naysayer on the society's course.

Challenge, though, tends to sort one's priorities. When I found myself engaged on tasks essential to preservation of our society and its values, my priorities sorted quickly and decisively. It brought me to the realization that by striving for and assuring the success of the private corporation, we are contributing to the success of our society. I have been determined ever since to work for the livable course over the long pull for everybody.

I regret that present generations have not all had comparable experiences. When we have not had large challenges to sort our priorities, it is easy to become persuaded that society is a nuisance, government a bother, and change only a burden and care.

In truth, of course, today's managers do face large challenges, perhaps the largest ever — for those challenges are no longer limited by national boundaries. They call us to serve the interests of all societies everywhere. That is why, in these reflections, I have tried to point our direction upward.

Today's corporation is, as corporations have always been, a concentration of capital supporting the plants and jobs and equipment needed to produce goods and provide services. Today's corporation is, though, as corporations never were before, a concentration of knowledge, of learned men and women, who, together, epitomize the higher values and civility to which we have come in this century. As such, today's corporation is, or ought to be, a center of the best that is within us, exerting constructive influence beyond one community and even one country to other continents and cultures.

That is why we must not permit times such as these to turn us from the constructive course. Change may be closing in on us from all sides, but we can cope with it — not by arguing against it, but by responding to it. That is the role and responsibility of the changing manager.